THINK FOR YOURSELF

A Kid's Guide to Solving Life's Dilemmas and Other Sticky Problems

CYNTHIA MACGREGOR

Lobster Press™

Think for Yourself:
A Kid's Guide to Solving Life's Dilemmas and Other Sticky Problems

Text © 2008 Cynthia MacGregor
Illustrations © 2008 Paula Becker

2nd Edition Published in 2008 by Lobster Press™
1620 Sherbrooke Street West, Suites C & D
Montréal, Québec H3H 1C9
Tel. (514) 904-1100 • Fax (514) 904-1101 • www.lobsterpress.com

Publisher: Alison Fripp
Editors: Meghan Nolan & William Mersereau
Editorial Assistant: Emma Stephen
Production Manager: Tammy Desnoyers
Design and Typesetting: Strong Finish Editorial and Design

We acknowledge the financial support of the Government of Canada through the
Book Publishing Industry Development Program (BPIDP) for our publishing activities.

The Canada Council | Le Conseil des Arts
for the Arts | du Canada

We acknowledge the support of the Canada Council
for the Arts for our publishing program.

Société
de développement
des entreprises
culturelles
Québec

We acknowledge the support of the government of Québec,
tax credit for book publishing, administered by SODEC.

Library and Archives Canada Cataloguing in Publication

MacGregor, Cynthia
    Think for yourself : a kid's guide to solving life's dilemmas and other sticky problems /
by Cynthia MacGregor ; illustrator: Paula Becker.

ISBN 978-1-897073-90-2

    1. Ethics – Juvenile literature. 2. Children – Conduct of life – Juvenile literature.
I. Becker, Paula, 1958- II. Title.

BJ1631.M33 2008   j170.83   C2008-901121-X

Printed and bound in Canada.

Text is printed on Rolland Enviro 100 Book,
100% recycled post-consumer fibre.

For Justin, Tori, Steffan, Aiden, Brian,
and Jayden — with love from Nana.
— Cynthia MacGregor

TABLE OF CONTENTS

INTRODUCTION

Uh oh.

How many times have you said that to yourself? And don't you hate the feeling that goes with it? That "uh oh" feeling comes when you're facing a *dilemma* — a word meaning a problem that you don't have an answer for right away. A "What-am-I-supposed-to-do-now?" problem.

Life is full of problems, isn't it? Small ones. Big ones. Sometimes you know what the answer is to a problem. Maybe you don't *like* the answer, but you know what you're *supposed* to do. Like when your friend asks you to help him cheat on a test. You know you're supposed to say no. The problem here is finding a way to say it without seeming like a bad friend. This is what is called a dilemma.

The idea behind this book is to help you learn how to deal with life's dilemmas. Because everyone's life is different, I can't think of every problem you're likely to encounter. In the following pages, I give you examples of some common dilemmas for kids your age and then provide you with some suggestions on how to solve them. Hopefully then, the next time you are faced with a dilemma of your own, you can remember some of these problem-solving techniques.

No matter what your dilemma might be, here are four key things to remember whenever that "uh oh" feeling takes over:

1– Accept the problem you have. Ignoring it isn't going to make it go away. And to put off dealing with it will actually make it worse in some cases.

2– Think about the possible ways to deal with it and then decide if one of these is the right way.

3– Have the courage to act on your decision to solve this dilemma.

4– And finally, be sure to congratulate yourself. Dealing with problems or dilemmas is *never* easy.

Now, what are the kinds of dilemmas you mostly face?

- Some are manners problems. Here, I'm referring to things like having to find a polite way thank someone for something you don't like without hurting their feelings. I don't mean stuff like remembering to say "please" or to use a tissue and not your sleeve to wipe your nose.
- Some are what you might call moral problems. By this I mean situations where you should not do things you think — or know — are wrong. The example I gave earlier of a friend asking you to help him cheat on a test is this kind of dilemma. Sometimes you're not sure what the right thing is to do. Other times you're pretty sure of what you need to do — or not do — but it's tough to figure out how to go about doing it (or not doing it).
- Some dilemmas fall into other categories, or they are a combination of manners and morals.

Dealing with the Dilemma

Sometimes the best way to solve a dilemma is to take apart the problem in your mind. Ask yourself:

- Just what is the dilemma?

- Why is it a dilemma?
- Maybe you think of a solution. Great. But what if you realize it isn't a good one? If that's the case, what is the problem with that solution?
- Now that you've figured out what's wrong with your solution, is there a way to get around the problem so that it will make the solution a better one? Maybe you're onto something and you just need to fine-tune it a little.

Wouldn't it be great if your school had a class in dilemma-solving? Well, this book can help you learn how to solve life's dilemmas and sticky situations . . . and there are no pop quizzes or grades involved!

Now let's look at some real-life dilemmas and see what possible solutions you might come up with.

PART 1

DILEMMAS WITH YOUR FRIENDS

DILEMMA 1

You are invited to a party at your friend's house. You know that boys *and* girls will be there. Your mom asks if there is going to be a parent present, and you ask your friend. Your friend says yes. However, when you get to the party, her parents aren't there. They have left your friend's older sister – who is sixteen – to supervise the party.

Why is this a dilemma?

You know that your mother believes there is a parent supervising the party — and you know that this is important to her because she had asked you if a parent was going to be there . . . and you said yes. Your mother probably wouldn't approve of you being at the party with only a sixteen-year-old in charge.

If you think of a solution, but it isn't a good one, what is the problem with that solution?

You could stay at the party and be extra sure not to do anything your parents would disapprove of. And then when you got home, you could plan to tell your mom that there was no parent present at the party after all, but that you were careful not to do anything wrong. However, you know that your mom probably doesn't want you to be at the party without proper parental supervision.

Is there a way around the problem?

The best thing to do is to call your parents as soon as you realize there are no parents at the party. Tell them honestly what the situation is. Ask if you can stay and then promise that you won't do anything they'd disapprove of. Promise, too, that you'll call them if the party gets out of hand or if you feel uncomfortable at all. Then ask if they'll let you stay at the party under those circumstances. Maybe they'll respect you for your honesty in calling them and they'll let you stay at least part of the evening. If not, and they insist that you come right home, you'll still have earned their trust by calling them and letting them know about the situation.

DILEMMA 2

A kid you really don't enjoy talking to or don't have anything in common with wants to be friends with you. She keeps inviting you over to her house after school.

Why is this a dilemma?

You don't have the same interests, or you just don't enjoy her company. However, she won't take no for an answer and keeps asking you. You don't want to just come out and say, "I don't want to spend time with you." You know that would hurt her feelings. But she keeps inviting you.

If you think of a solution, but it isn't a good one, what is the problem with that solution?

You could say yes just once, to be polite. But then if she has fun hanging out with you, she's likely to ask to spend time with you more often than ever. And if you don't have a good time, the problem will have only gotten worse.

Is there a way around the problem?

If you just don't like this girl, you'll have to keep saying no until she gets the message that you don't want to spend time with her after school. It's always a good idea to be polite to people and not hurt their feelings unnecessarily. This means that you should *not* just come out and tell her you don't like her. But it doesn't mean you have to spend time with her just to keep from hurting her feelings.

Then again, maybe you're not sure whether you really dislike her or not. Maybe you just don't enjoy doing the same things. If that's the case, you could try showing her the things you like. Maybe she could learn to like playing the games you like to play. Maybe she could learn to like doing the things you like to do. Maybe *you* could even learn to like doing some of the things *she* enjoys. It's worth trying once. And if it doesn't work out, you have a very good reason to say "No thank you" the next time she invites you over. You could say: "I'm sorry, but I don't like biking and you don't like playing computer games. I don't enjoy the TV shows you like and you don't like the TV shows I like. You don't like playing volleyball and I don't like playing soccer. We just don't like doing the same things."

Here's something else to consider: maybe she doesn't have enough friends. Is there someone else you know who likes the same things she likes? Maybe you could suggest she make after-school plans with this other girl? Maybe your friend Ashley would love to be friends with her? Even if you don't particularly enjoy spending time with her, maybe Ashley would. Even if you don't like doing the things she likes, maybe Ashley does. You'll do her a favor by finding her a friend *and* you'll be able to distance yourself from her.

DILEMMA 3

You and your friend find a wallet on the street. *You* want to either try to find the owner and return it to him, or turn it in to the police. *Your friend* looks through the wallet and wants to keep the money. He says, "We're not stealing. We found it on the street. If we hadn't found it, someone else would have. And they would have kept the money. So we're not doing anything wrong."

Why is this a dilemma?

If you insist on returning the wallet and money, then your friend isn't going to be very happy with you. If you give in to him and agree to take the money, then you aren't going to be very happy with yourself.

If you think of a solution, but it isn't a good one, what is the problem with that solution?

You could let your friend keep the wallet and all the money. That way you yourself aren't guilty of keeping something that isn't yours. But you still would know that someone somewhere is looking for the wallet she lost. And *you* know where that wallet is, but you aren't doing anything about returning it to its rightful owner. And, since you didn't keep any of the money yourself, your friend is still likely to rub it in that you're a wimp.

Is there a way around the problem?

Somebody's going to be unhappy with somebody no matter how you work this out. So isn't it better for you to try to see that the money is returned? That way, even if your friend is unhappy with you, at least you'll feel good about yourself. And the owner of the wallet will be relieved.

But maybe with a little smart thinking you can get your friend to see things your way. It's worth a try. Tell him, "What if *you* lost your wallet and it had all of your allowance money in it? Wouldn't you like the person who found it to return it to you? Don't you think we should do the same thing for the person who lost this wallet?"

You can even add, "Who knows, maybe this person really needs the money? But even if she doesn't, it is *her* money, not ours. We need to try to find her in order to return it." And you can also say, "You never know — maybe there'll be a reward. Now *that* would be money we could keep with a clear conscience." Explain that no matter what, you will both sleep better at night knowing that you did the right thing to help the person who lost her wallet.

DILEMMA 4

You've made plans with a friend for Friday night. She's going to sleep over, and you plan to watch a movie and stay up late. Her mom doesn't let her go to sleepovers very often, so she has been looking forward to this for three weeks. Then your best friend calls you. She has two free tickets to a musical you've been dying to see and she wants you to go with her – on the same night as your sleepover with your other friend. The musical is only going to be in town for three days and the tickets are usually really expensive and difficult to get.

Why is this a dilemma?

You *really* want to go to the musical with your best friend, but you've already promised your other friend you'd have a sleepover to spend time with her that night.

If you think of a solution, but it isn't a good one, what is the problem with that solution?

You could ask your best friend if your other friend could go to the show too. But your best friend explains that she was only able to get two tickets. You could ask your best friend to join you and your other friend for the sleepover; but if your best friend has complimentary tickets, she probably can't trade them in for tickets on a different date.

Is there a way around the problem?

There's no perfect solution here. You're going to disappoint one friend ... and you're going to be disappointed yourself ... no matter what you choose. You have to either stick with your initial commitment and disappoint your best friend, or disappoint your other friend by canceling and then going to the musical with your best friend.

But it's important to remember that a commitment is a commitment. You know deep down that it's better to stick to your plan with your other friend since you made that plan first. You might be disappointed because you really wanted to see the show ... but it was bad timing. Thank your best friend for the offer and explain that you'd love to go, but that you've already made plans with your other friend that night. Ask your best friend to get an extra program for you and tell her you can't wait to hear all about the show afterward. Then turn your attention to the sleepover. Your other friend is counting on — and looking forward to — spending time with you. And she doesn't get to go to many sleepovers, which makes this special for her. So it's best to put the musical out of your mind and to have fun hanging out with your friend. (Just be sure not mention the tickets you had to turn down as this might make her feel guilty, and you don't want that.) You might feel bad about missing out on the musical, but in the long run, you'll feel better about being a good friend.

DILEMMA 5

Your friend tells you, "You've got to see what I found on the internet!" It turns out he's talking about a porn site. Your parents have told you they don't want you visiting that type of Web site. In fact, they have software on your computer that prevents that type of site and related images from being displayed on your screen. But your friend's parents don't have any controls like this on their computer.

Why is this a dilemma?

Your friend's got you curious. You've never seen anything like this before. In addition, you don't want to look like a baby by saying, "My parents won't let me."

If you think of a solution, but it isn't a good one, what is the problem with that solution?

If your friend accessed the site, and you were only looking over his shoulder, then technically it wouldn't be *you* who visited the site. Or maybe your friend could print out some of the pictures and give them to you. That way you'd get a sampling of what's on the site without actually going to the site yourself.

But you know that your parents really don't want you looking at this type of material at all. Even if you're not the one who accessed the site. Even if you're not viewing the pictures while on the internet but are looking at them on printouts.

Is there a way around the problem?

The only right thing to do is not get involved. You might want to look – curiosity is natural. But certain images could make you feel uncomfortable and you might have lots questions – things you might not want to share with your friend. Plus, you don't want to break your parents' trust. They have lots of reasons for not wanting you to see these types of images on your computer at home. Explain to your friend that you'd rather check out sports scores online, or play a computer game. This way, you still have fun hanging out with him, and you don't have to worry about feeling uncomfortable. Then when you see your parents later, you don't have to feel guilty about doing something behind their backs that they wouldn't agree with.

DILEMMA 6

You go to a friend's birthday party and find that some of the kids there brought alcohol and are secretly drinking it in the basement.

Why is this a dilemma?

Alcohol at the party presents three big problems. One: it's illegal — you and your friends are all underage. If somehow the police find out there is alcohol at this party, you could get in trouble too. Two: you are scared. What if these kids get out of control? Or what if they pressure you to drink? Three: your parents would be extremely upset if they knew you were at a party where kids were drinking alcohol.

If you think of a solution, but it isn't a good one, what is the problem with that solution?

You could stay at the party and just refuse to drink any alcohol your-self. But you know that your parents would still be upset that you were there because the situation could be dangerous—kids your age can't handle drinking. They could get really sick and/or they could do some-thing really stupid. Even with only a little bit of alcohol, things might get out of hand. It really isn't a safe place for you to be.

Is there a way around the problem?

You really need to leave the party — and not just to please your parents. Kids and alcohol don't mix. You need to leave *for your own safety*. Things could get messy, and you don't want to be in the middle of it . . . or be a victim. Call your parents, tell them what's going on, and ask them to come and get you. They'll respect you for it.

DILEMMA 7

Your friend shoplifts sometimes. Your mom has always told you that stealing is wrong. Your friend says, "I wouldn't steal from a person. This is different. I'm stealing from a big company. They expect some people to steal. My dad said so. Come with me. We can take some magazines. They'll never catch us. It's fun and it's free!" When you say no, she calls you a wimp.

Why is this a dilemma?

Nobody likes to be called names. But you know deep down that stealing is wrong — *any* kind of stealing.

If you think of a solution, but it isn't a good one, what is the problem with that solution?

You could go along with your friend's plan and walk out of the store with the magazines. You could then read the magazines, without messing them up at all, and then mail them back to the store without your name on the envelope. You could enclose a note saying you didn't want to take them and you're returning them now. That way, the store would have them back and could sell them.

But you're still doing something wrong. And you might even get caught. (Don't forget, stores are getting better and better technology to cut down on theft.) And even if you don't get caught, your friend will only want to do the same thing all over again another time. So you really haven't solved anything in the long run.

Is there a way around the problem?

You can point out to your friend that stealing is stealing, whether you're stealing from a person or a big company. (Even big companies are still owned by people.) You can also point out that when people steal from stores, it costs the stores money. In order to make back the money that they lose from theft, stores have to raise their prices. So by stealing from the store, you're making the prices go up and in a way, you still have to pay for it.

Maybe your friend will see it your way. Maybe your friend will realize now that any stealing is wrong. But even if your friend doesn't agree with you, even if she still wants to steal or says you're not being a friend, or that you're being a wuss, you need to stand up for what you know is right and do what you know is right.

What's right is to not steal. What's right is to try to make your friend understand that too. If you walk out of the store without taking anything, and you've tried to keep your friend from stealing, you've done the right thing. This is true regardless of what your friend winds up doing. Maybe someday she will eventually see things your way. In any event, she will know not to try to get you involved in shoplifting the next time you're together.

DILEMMA 8

All your friends download music and movies from the internet and buy video games at cheap prices. Your parents have pointed out to you that when you download music and movies that way, you're often stealing copyrighted material, and that the low-priced video games are often "pirated" copies. They have asked you not to download music or movies illegally or buy games that way anymore.

Why is this a dilemma?

Your parents are always on your case to save money. And you don't want to have to spend all your allowance on CDs, movies, or video games. None of your friends do. They all download music and movies, and they buy less-expensive copies of games. It seems your choices are to download from the internet against your parents' wishes, to spend *all* your money on CDs, or to do without a nice collection of movies, music, and games.

If you think of a solution, but it isn't a good one, what is the problem with that solution?

You could copy your friends' CDs and movies. That way, you're not downloading from the internet sites that your parents asked you to keep away from. However, while you're following the *exact words* of what they said, you know you're not really avoiding what they want you to avoid. You're still pirating.

Is there a way around the problem?

The music company, the recording artist (singer or group), the person who wrote the song . . . they all get paid for each CD sold. The actors, the director, the writers who wrote the script . . . they all get paid for each DVD sold. And those video games? Somebody wrote the code for those games, and that person needs to get paid too. People worked really hard to make something you like, and they deserve to be paid for it. If nobody bought these games, movies, and music, nobody would earn any money, and people would stop writing and recording songs, making movies, and creating new video games.

There are a few things that you can do. The first is to buy the DVD, game, or CD. You don't need to buy *every* CD, movie, or video game you want though. Be selective. Get only the ones that you really, *really* like and can afford. After all, you don't want to save up for a movie that you will only watch once or a game that is too easy. Remember, you can always rent games and movies for a few dollars, or borrow DVDs and CDs from the library. This lets you try them out and determine if you really like something. Then you can save up to buy your own copy when you are sure you want it.

You can also ask your parents and friends if they know of any stores that let you trade your old CDs, DVDs, or games for new ones. That way, when you have listened to a CD, watched a movie, or beaten a game, you can switch it for something you haven't tried yet. These stores have games, music, and movies that other people owned and are now finished with, so even if you don't have something to trade, you can probably buy what you want at a low price that is still fair.

DILEMMA 9

You're sitting in the lunchroom with a bunch of your friends, and a classmate walks in. This girl wears clothes that your friends think are weird. She wears shirts and skirts or shirts and pants that just don't go together. She sometimes wears clothes that have been patched and look old. Her shoes are funny looking and don't go with the clothes she's wearing. The other girls start talking about her. You think they're talking loudly enough that she can hear them.

Why is this a dilemma?

Even though you're not this girl's friend, you don't dislike her. Even though you agree that she dresses in a different way, you think it might not be her fault. Maybe her parents can't afford to buy her new clothes and shoes. You really don't want to talk negatively about her behind her back — plus, she can probably hear what the girls are saying since they're being so loud. But if you tell the other girls to be quiet, they'll just say, "What's your problem? Since when are you *her* friend?"

If you think of a solution, but it isn't a good one, what is the problem with that solution?

You could get up and leave the table. Then you wouldn't be part of the group that's talking about this girl and hurting her feelings. And nobody would put you down, either. But the other girls would keep on talking, your classmate would still hear them, and her feelings would still be hurt.

Is there a way around the problem?

You could be really bold and brave and start a conversation about people who are different and people who might not have a lot of money. You could say something like, "You know, we're pretty lucky that we have certain things. Plus, it's okay to be different. It would be pretty boring if everyone was the same. And anyway, everyone has different taste." Try to get your friends to imagine themselves in this girl's place, and try to put things in perspective for them.

DILEMMA 10

Your best friend, Joey, is running for class president. You really like your best buddy, but you think that his opponent, Kevin Matthews, would be a better class president. The next time you see Joey, he says, "You're voting for me, right?"

Why is this a dilemma?

Joey thinks you'll vote for him because you're best friends. You know Kevin is really the better choice. Do you vote for Kevin and get your best friend mad at you? Do you vote for Joey and know you're doing it for the wrong reasons?

If you think of a solution, but it isn't a good one, what is the problem with that solution?

You could vote for Kevin and tell Joey that you voted for him. The voting is secret; he'll never know. Or you could vote for Joey. What's one vote? If Kevin is the better person for class president, he'll probably win anyhow.

There are two problems here: First, you are lying. Second, you are not doing what you want to do or what you feel would be best.

Is there a way around the problem?

If Kevin is the better person for the job, you should vote for Kevin. If everyone votes for their friends, this will turn into a popularity contest.

But it's not a popularity contest; it's an election for an important school office.

You don't have to tell Joey who you are going to vote for — and you don't have to lie, either. You can learn to be evasive in a diplomatic way. When Joey asks, "Who did you vote for?" you can answer by laughing and saying, "Who do you think I voted for?" You didn't come right out and say you voted for him. You didn't lie. If he pushes for more, you can say, "My vote went to the best person for the job, of course," and smile at him. You've saved his feelings, not hurt them. Yet, you've voted for the best person and didn't outright lie to Joey. Yes, it's a little less than honest . . . but it's not *dis*honest. And you haven't hurt anyone's feelings, which is important. Plus, you've done what your conscience told you was right.

DILEMMA 11

Your friend didn't study for the big math test that is happening today. You almost always get As in math. Now your friend wants you to pass him the answers so he won't fail.

Why is this a dilemma?

You don't want to be a cheater, but you don't want to seem as if you're a bad friend. You also don't want your friend to be mad at you — if you refuse to help him, he won't be very happy with you.

If you think of a solution, but it isn't a good one, what is the problem with that solution?

You could cheat, to be a good friend, but you might get caught. Even if you didn't get caught, you wouldn't feel very good about yourself.

You could refuse to help him, and you could tell him it's his own fault if he didn't study. But you know he doesn't want a lecture from you.

Is there a way around the problem?

You could tell him that the reason why you won't cheat is because if you get caught, then you'll be in trouble. You could then explain that you don't want him to fail the test, but if you get caught cheating, the teacher will fail you too. Point out to him that that wouldn't be fair to you. Now you're not lecturing him, and you're not refusing only because it's wrong to cheat. You're protecting yourself. He should understand that a bit better.

Maybe you can offer to help him some other way. You could suggest going over a few math problems with him quickly before school starts. Maybe you could help him study for the next test if he doesn't like studying alone.

By offering something in return, you're not just flatly refusing to help him. You're showing that *you* are being a good friend. And if he's really a friend, then he's probably a lot less likely to be angry if you take this approach.

DILEMMA 12

You're friends in school with a guy named Noah. Another guy, Rich, bullies Noah whenever there aren't any adults around to see him and stop him. Rich is bigger and stronger than Noah, who is short and thin. Rich does mean stuff like push Noah, throw his books on the floor, and call Noah names. He also threatens to physically harm Noah. He never has actually hit or kicked him, but Noah is afraid.

Noah will not tell his parents about Rich. He says his father would get mad at him for not standing up for himself. Plus, he doesn't want people to think he's a wimp.

Why is this a dilemma?

You don't like the way Rich bullies Noah, and you're afraid that one of these days he'll actually beat Noah up or do something else to him that's worse than what he's done already. You want to do something to help Noah, but you don't know what to do.

If you think of a solution, but it isn't a good one, what is the problem with that solution?

You could come to Noah's defense next time Rich does something to him. With two of you standing up to Rich, you might be able to stop him. But then Rich would have it in for you too, and you don't know what he might do to you. You've already seen the mean things he's done to Noah.

Or you could go behind Noah's back and tell his parents what's going on. But you don't really know them.

Is there a way around the problem?

If your school has peer mediators or peer counselors, you can bring the matter to them. Let them take up the issue since they have authority.

If your school has no peer mediators or peer counselors, you could still talk to a bunch of the other kids in your class, or in your school. You could get them to agree to talk to Rich as a group. They can then warn him that if he messes with Noah again, they'll *all* be really angry with him. If Rich knows that that many kids are watching what he does to Noah, he might leave Noah alone.

And if that doesn't work, talk to a teacher or to the principal and let them know what is happening.

DILEMMA 13

As you're walking home from the school bus stop, one of your friends pulls out a pack of cigarettes and offers you one.

Why is this a dilemma?

You know how bad smoking is — you've learned all about the many ways it can really hurt your body. And who wants to reek of cigarette smoke? Plus, your parents would freak out if they caught you smoking. However, you don't want your friend to make fun of you or think you're a wimp for not giving it a try.

If you think of a solution, but it isn't a good one, what is the problem with that solution?

You could take a quick puff or two and make sure not to inhale the smoke into your lungs. That way, your friend won't get on your case. But there are two problems with this. One: trying the cigarette might make you cough or feel as if you want to throw up — even if you try not to inhale. And what if your friend expects you to smoke all the time with him? Two: a neighbor might see you and tell your parents.

Is there a way around the problem?

It's important to take a stand and firmly decline the offer. You don't have to justify your decision on the basis of "My parents wouldn't want

me to." Instead, stick to health reasons for refusing. You can say, "Cancer? No thanks. I don't want any." Or you can say, "If you want to risk your health, that's your business, but *I* know what cigarettes can do to you." Or, "No thanks, I'd rather not smell like an ashtray." And if you play any sports, you can add, "Besides, cigarettes leave you winded. It wouldn't be good for my soccer game." Then, ask your friend not to smoke around you. If he doesn't know the dangers of second-hand smoke, fill him in nicely. If he's a true friend, he'll respect your request to protect your health.

DILEMMA 14

Some older kids are always selling drugs on the corner near your school. So far, you've avoided these kids, but today they approach you and your friends.

Why is this a dilemma?

You know that taking drugs can kill you. And you've heard all about how easy it is to get hooked if you try it and like it.

And beyond the problem of what the drugs themselves do to you, there's another problem. Drugs are illegal. If you get caught with drugs in your possession, you'll be in huge trouble — trouble with the police, trouble with your family, and perhaps trouble with your school. You could wind up in jail. You could wind up with a criminal record. You could wind up causing irreparable damage to your life.

Drugs aren't a good thing for another reason, too: People who take drugs are sometimes driven to commit crimes in order to get the drugs they want or to get the money they need in order to buy the drugs. The more drug dealers and drug takers you have around a neighborhood, the more unsafe and unpleasant that neighborhood is. Do you want bad stuff happening near where you and your family live?

If you think of a solution, but it isn't a good one, what is the problem with that solution?

You and your friends could say no to the dealer. But the dealer might try to do something to you in order to get even. You could just ignore him, and you and your friends could promise each other not to buy any drugs. But you know some other kids might be curious and may then buy them. Plus, you know that people who deal and/or do drugs can be dangerous, and you want your neighborhood and school to stay safe.

Is there a way around the problem?

This is one of those dilemmas that you need an adult to help solve. You can't fix this problem yourself, but you can play a big part in solving it by alerting an adult who can do something. After you tell the kid who wants to give you drugs, "No, I don't want any," then quickly walk away and try to find someone appropriate to report the dealer to — like your parents, the school principal, the police, or even the crossing guard if there is one nearby. Then let them handle the situation from there.

What if it happens that the dealer is a friend of one of your friends? Then don't tell your friends you're reporting the dealer. No one ever has to know it was you. Do it quietly. **But do it.** You know how bad drugs are and what they can do to people — you don't want drugs in your community.

DILEMMA 15

You suddenly realize that you've made plans to meet with two friends for the same day. When David invited you to come over after school Tuesday and you agreed, you totally forgot that you'd already made plans with Scott for that same afternoon. What a mess! You weren't trying to hurt anyone's feelings, but now it looks as if you're going to have to cancel on someone.

Why is this a dilemma?

You want to see both friends. You don't want to hurt David's feelings by saying you're getting together with Scott, but you don't want to hurt Scott's feelings by saying you're going over to David's house.

If you think of a solution, but it isn't a good one, what is the problem with that solution?

You could cancel your plans with both of them and reschedule for a different day, but then you might hurt their feelings . . . *and* you mess up your own afternoon.

Is there a way around the problem?

If your parents say it's okay for you to have two friends over on Tuesday afternoon, you could tell both David and Scott that you messed up and made two sets of plans for the same day. Then explain that you'd like them both to come to your house instead.

But maybe your folks said no. Or maybe David and Scott don't get along well together. In that case, you have to figure out which friend you made the plans with first. Then you have to tell the other one that you're sorry, but you messed up and you need to reschedule your plans for some other time.

People make honest mistakes, and this was one. Nobody should get angry with you over it.

DILEMMA 16

Your friend has met another kid, Travis, online. Travis has a lot of the same interests your friend has. He and Travis have become great buddies online. Travis says he wants to get together with your friend to show him his prized baseball card collection. But your friend's parents are very strict. They wouldn't approve of him hanging out with someone they've never met, so your friend decides to meet Travis somewhere else. Your friend tells you about his plans, but he asks you to keep it a secret so that his parents don't get mad.

Why is this a dilemma?

You know that there are some people with bad intentions on the internet. You know that sometimes online, people pretend to be people they aren't: adults pose as kids, or boys pose as girls, etc. Travis might really be just who he says he is. He might really be a kid who wants to show your friend his baseball card collection. But on the other hand, he might be an adult who is trying to trick your friend. This person might be a predator.

You explain all of this to your friend. But he says he's sure Travis is okay. He insists he's going to meet Travis in the park on Friday. And he's not worried about anything. He says you worry too much.

If you think of a solution, but it isn't a good one, what is the problem with that solution?

You could hide somewhere in the park and try to keep an eye on your friend. You could make sure that Travis really is a kid and that everything is OK. If you see something that looks strange, something dangerous, you could try to rescue your buddy. But if something goes wrong, you might not be able to help him — especially if Travis *is* really a grown man. And if Travis is really a bad guy, something bad could happen to you, too.

Is there a way around the problem?

You need to tell your friend to invite Travis over to his house, while his parents are home, so that they can meet him. But make sure that your friend's parents make that decision. Let them decide if they even want him to give Travis his home address.

If this doesn't work, then tell an adult. Yes, your friend will probably be mad at you. But which is worse: having him mad at you or having something bad happen? If Travis is really a kid and he really is okay, he shouldn't mind going to your friend's house and meeting his parents. If you aren't comfortable telling your buddy's parents what's going on, tell an adult. Tell a teacher, the principal, or your own mom or dad. But don't let your friend go alone to meet someone he met on the internet.

DILEMMA 17

You and your family have moved, and you are now attending a new school. But you don't fit in there. The kids have different interests from your old friends back home. You haven't met anyone you'd like to be friends with or even hang out with.

Why is this a dilemma?

You miss your old friends to begin with. And not having made any new friends, you miss your old friends even more. You know that you're supposed to be going to school to learn, not to have fun. But you also know that school isn't supposed to be a total grind. You're supposed to enjoy yourself during lunch hour and after school with the friends you meet in class.

If you think of a solution, but it isn't a good one, what is the problem with that solution?

You could ask your parents to send you to a private school in a nearby town. Maybe you would find kids there who would share more of your interests. But most private schools are expensive, and your parents really aren't rich.

Or you could ask them to let you go live with Grandma, back home. Then you could go to your old school. But then you'd miss your parents, and you know they'd miss you too.

Is there a way around the problem?

Ask your parents to help you find one or more clubs or groups for kids who have the same interests you do. What are you interested in? Playing softball or soccer or some other sport? Playing chess? Playing video games? Debating? Reading graphic novels? Working out? Playing the guitar?

If you join a club or other group for kids with the same interest, you're halfway toward solving the problem. Surely, among all the kids in that club, you'll find several people you like.

Since you probably have more than one interest, you ought to be able to find more than one club you can join. This will give you extra opportunities to meet kids you like and who enjoy the same things you do. Some organizations for kids, of course, are extracurricular clubs that are offered by the school. But the local Y or community center, a gym, an arts organization, or some other group also may have a club or other group for kids with your interests.

Have your parents check the newspaper, ask their neighbors and new friends, and ask anywhere else they can think of. (They could try calling your town's visitors' bureau or Leisure Services Department, too.) *You* can help as well! Do a Web search for the things you're interested in. In a search engine, enter "guitar" and your town's name and take it from there. See what you turn up.

You may even meet kids who go to your own school this way . . . they might be a year older or younger than you, but they could share your interests and your values. And even if they go to a different school, it will still be nice to make new friends who you can really relate to.

DILEMMA 18

A new girl, Lisa, recently transferred to your school. She's really nice and really fun. At first you made friends with her because you felt bad – she was sitting by herself at lunch, ignored by the other girls before and after classes, and was generally alone. You knew that couldn't feel very good.

But as you started spending time with her, you found you really liked her. She's a fun person, a nice person, and an interesting one, too. You really enjoy her company. You invited her over to your house and you had a great afternoon together.

You thought your best friend, Marie, would like her, too, so you introduced the two of them. But to your surprise – and to your dismay – Marie didn't take to Lisa at all. She's actually acting jealous now!

Why is this a dilemma?

You don't want to lose your best friend. But you also don't want to turn your back on Lisa. To begin with, you don't want to hurt her feelings. And on top of that, you really enjoy spending time with her. You don't want to lose her friendship. What can you do?

If you think of a solution, but it isn't a good one, what is the problem with that solution?

You can tell Marie to stop acting like a baby. You can point out that this isn't a case of either/or. You don't have to choose between friends. You have other friends. Why is Marie getting so put out by your being friends with Lisa?

But Marie isn't acting rationally. She isn't being sensible. And telling her to stop acting like a baby isn't going to make things better. In fact, it might make her really angry with you. Then she might stop talking to you. You don't want that!

Is there a way around the problem?

Instead of pointing out to Marie that she's being unreasonable, appeal to her kind side. (After all, she must have a good heart or you wouldn't have chosen her as a best friend in the first place!) Ask her to put herself in Lisa's place. How would Marie feel if *she* were in a new school and didn't know anyone? How would she like it if only one person had made friends with her?

Tell Marie that Lisa needs her help. Tell Marie that the new girl really needs some friends, and you just know that Marie could be a good friend to Lisa. Then leave it up to Marie as to whether she wants to spend time with Lisa one-on-one or invite Lisa to join the two of you when you spend time together.

By suggesting that Marie spend time with Lisa, you're not making it seem that you're spending less time with Marie because of the new girl. After all, maybe your best friend does feel a little threatened. We all have times when we worry about losing a friendship.

DILEMMA 19

You studied the script for the school play very hard before the auditions. You really, really, *really* wanted the lead. But so did a very good friend of yours . . . and she ended up getting picked over you. You got a part in the play, but not a good one. Now your friend wants you to help her learn her lines.

Why is this a dilemma?

Maybe your friend really doesn't mean to rub it in that she got the lead and you didn't. But you know that helping her learn her lines is only going to make you feel worse. Still, she *is* your friend. And you don't want to look like a sore loser. But you also don't want to do something that will make you feel even more jealous.

If you think of a solution, but it isn't a good one, what is the problem with that solution?

You could tell her you have too much homework and can't help her. But if she's in your class, she knows how much homework you have. Even if you're in different classes, she might find out you don't really have that much homework. Besides, you know you shouldn't lie. And even if you get out of helping her today, isn't she likely to ask you again tomorrow? It might take her a week or more to learn her lines.

Is there a way around the problem?

Be honest. Tell her that you're very happy that she got the part she wanted. But tell her that, at the same time, you're also feeling bad because you didn't get the part — and that you really wanted it too! And tell her that it would only make you feel worse to help her learn the lines for the part you wanted so much. Tell her you don't want to do anything that might make you feel resentful toward her. You value your friendship with her too much for that! So ask her if she could enlist the help of one of her other friends to help her learn the lines. That way, you won't start feeling jealous or resentful of your good friend.

DILEMMA 20

Evan, a boy you don't like, has invited you to his birthday party.

Why is this a dilemma?

If you don't go, you may hurt Evan's feelings, and you'd feel bad about doing that. When you have birthday parties, you want everyone to come, so you know how Evan would feel if you said you couldn't go.

If you think of a solution, but it isn't a good one, what is the problem with that solution?

You can go anyhow — two or three hours wouldn't be so awful. But then maybe Evan will expect you to invite him to your next party — and to make occasional after-school plans with him as well.

Is there a way around the problem?

If this is a party to which all of the class, or a lot of other kids, have been invited, you might want to go. Since it's not a one-on-one situation, you don't need to spend lots of time alone with Evan. And since many kids will be there, Evan can't expect all of you to become good friends with him after the party has taken place. But if you know that not many kids were invited, you might be better off saying "No thanks."

In any event, you would need to check with your parents first. Tell them you've been invited to a party you don't want to go to. Ask your mom or dad to tell you they have other plans for you that day. When one of them does, you can tell Evan that your parents said no because you are supposed to be doing something else that day. (But be sure to wish him a happy birthday!) The "something else" might just be your homework, but *technically* you're not lying.

There are times when half-truths are kinder than the whole truth. Which is better: to say, "I have something else to do that day" (and then stay home to do your homework) or to say, "I don't really want to go to your party"? You may not like Evan, but you don't want to hurt his feelings unnecessarily.

You also don't want to just go to his party and then set up the expectation that now you're going to be good friends. So wiggling out of the invitation with a half-truth is the kindest thing you can do.

DILEMMA 21

Your friend has body odor. At the start of every school day, it's barely noticeable, but it's there. As the day goes on, it gets worse. By the time gym class is over, he's really stinky. He's a friend, but he's not your best buddy, so you feel kind of awkward mentioning it to him. On the other hand, it's no fun to smell him, either in school or after school . . . and he does like spending time with you after school.

Why is this a dilemma?

You don't like being around this guy because he *smells.* You'd like to spend more time with him. You both like shooting hoops. You both like playing video games. But he has a real odor problem. You're even starting to avoid him because of it. You know, or at least you are pretty sure, that some of the other kids are also avoiding him for the same reason.

If you think of a solution, but it isn't a good one, what is the problem with that solution?

You want to help him because he's your friend. If people were keeping away from you for a reason, you'd want someone to let you know. If you tell him he stinks and he needs to wash better, you'll hurt his feelings — even if you say it politely.

You could also leave him an anonymous note in his desk or locker that tells him he has an odor problem. But then he might wonder who left the note and he might start feeling self-conscious and embarrassed because of it. You don't want to embarrass him by telling him to his face. But when he looks at everyone in class and wonders, "Who's the person who left me that note?" he might be more embarrassed than ever. No one wants that. (That's also why you don't want to talk to the other kids about his odor problem when he's around. He might see or hear you whispering and might guess it's about him. He might even hear his name mentioned and *know* it's about him.)

Is there a way around the problem?

This is a tricky situation. If you know his mom or dad reasonably well, you could try to either go see one of them or call one of them on the phone — when you know your friend isn't home. To be safe, tell his parents, "Please don't call him to the phone — I'm calling to talk to you." Then tell the mom or dad what the problem is. Explain that you don't want to embarrass the guy by saying anything to him. Tell his mom or dad that you're sure some of the kids keep away from him because of his odor problem. It might be an awkward conversation, but his parents will be thankful for having the opportunity to intervene in order to help their son. Maybe they haven't noticed the problem. Knowing about it now may encourage them to buy him deodorant and explain to him how to use it. Or maybe his parents will make an extra effort to ensure his clothes get a good washing between uses. Involving his parents will end up helping him without embarrassing him. No one has to know that it was you who took action.

If you can't talk to the guy's parents, maybe your teacher would talk to him or to his parents. Speak with your teacher privately and see if he or she will help with the situation. In the end, everyone will be more comfortable around this kid, and he will surely have more fun when people aren't avoiding him.

DILEMMA 22

You go over to a friend's house to watch movies. When you get there, your friend's older brother and his friends are watching X-rated movies. They invite you to join them. You know your parents don't want you watching things like this.

Why is this a dilemma?

To begin with, you've never seen an X-rated movie, and maybe you're curious. Besides, if you say you won't watch because your parents wouldn't like it, your friend's brother and his friends might call you a baby.

If you think of a solution, but it isn't a good one, what is the problem with that solution?

You *could* watch the videos and just not tell your parents. Then you wouldn't get in trouble . . . and, after all, what's the big deal about watching a couple of movies? But if you did that, and your parents ever found out, they wouldn't trust you as much. Besides, you know you're not supposed to.

Is there a way around the problem?

You need to stand up for what you know is right, even if someone calls you a name. Tell the other kids, "Sorry, but I'm not allowed to watch X-rated movies." Then suggest to your friend that the two of you do something else while you wait for the television to be free.

But what if one of the kids wants to be mean and says something like, "Do you always do everything your *mommy* tells you?" You can then say, "I don't sneak behind my parents' backs. That's why they trust me. I've worked hard to earn their trust, and I'm not going to mess up now." Take pride in standing up for yourself. No matter what anyone says, you'll know deep down you're doing the right thing. And, no matter what the other kids say, they know it too!

DILEMMA 23

You're walking around the neighborhood with a friend. Suddenly, he opens his backpack and pulls out two spray cans of black paint. "Hey, you know the Johnsons' old house?" he says. "Let's paint GOODBYE AND GET LOST on the front door." You know the Johnsons' old house very well. It's around the corner from your house, and you were very glad when the Johnsons moved out. They were always mean to you and your friends. They didn't like kids. You were glad the day you saw the moving van in front of their house.

Why is this a dilemma?

You agree with the words your friend wants to paint on their front door. You're very glad the Johnsons moved out of the neighborhood. But you know that vandalism is both wrong and illegal. You know that if anyone sees you, or somehow finds out you did it, you'll be in big trouble.

If you think of a solution, but it isn't a good one, what is the problem with that solution?

You could tell your friend you don't want to get in trouble, so you won't do it. But then he might call you a wimp.

Is there a way around the problem?

Tell your friend you won't do it, but don't tell him it's because you are afraid of getting in trouble. Remind him that this is your neighborhood too. Tell him that when a house, storefront, or fence is spray-painted, it makes the whole neighborhood look bad and it costs a lot to clean up. Tell him you don't want to do that to your neighborhood.

You can also tell him this: Since the Johnsons don't live there anymore, maybe they don't own the house anymore. If somebody new owns the house, it's *their* door he's going to ruin, not the Johnsons'. That wouldn't be fair to the new owner, would it? The new owner never did anything mean to you. And if the new owners' door gets spray-painted, they might think all the kids in the neighborhood are bad. Then they won't treat you any better than the Johnsons did. So it's in your own best interests not to vandalize the house. (Consider this, too: If the new owner, or the police, ever finds out that you were the ones who vandalized the house, you're both going to have to pay for a new door. And that's going to take a good chunk of money. There goes that new bike or video game you were saving for.)

Now you're not saying no out of just plain worry. Now you're saying "No" to protect your neighborhood and to try to keep the new owners from being mean to you and your friends and to keep from having to pay for a new door. Mike should respect all these reasons. He has no reason now to call you names. And you've given him three very good reasons for not spray-painting the door.

DILEMMA 24

Your friend is over at your house, and you log on to your computer together. She says, "Hey, let's play a trick on Hanna." Hanna is a girl in your school neither of you likes because she thinks she's the most wonderful thing on Earth. Hanna really likes a guy named Brent. Your friend says you should pretend to be Brent and send Hanna a mean email. She says she knows how to get a free email account and make it look as if it belongs to Brent. "While we're at it," your friend adds, "I know something else we can do." She says Hanna belongs to a social networking site and that the two of you can pretend to be Brent on the site and then leave some really mean comments about Hanna there, too. "I bet she won't think she's so great after we do that," your friend says.

Why is this a dilemma?

You think it would be really satisfying to do something that would stop Hanna from thinking she's so much better than everyone else. But you're not sure about pretending to be someone you're not. One, you're not sure even Hanna deserves what your friend wants to do to her. Two, you might get Brent in trouble, and you don't want to do that, since Brent's a pretty nice kid. But your friend is eager to see her plan through, and she is not just your friend but your guest. You don't really want to create an uncomfortable situation.

If you think of a solution, but it isn't a good one, what is the problem with that solution?

You could pretend to be someone other than Brent, and that way at least Brent won't get in trouble. But you're still doing something that is unkind. And you know it isn't right to pretend to be someone you're not. It also really isn't right to be mean like that to Hanna, no matter what you and your friend think of her.

Is there a way around the problem?

You have to stand up for doing the right thing, which, in this case, is *not* being mean and *not* pretending to be someone else — *anyone* else — whether it's Brent or not. There are other fun things you and your friend can do together, online or offline, that don't involve hurting someone's feelings and reputation. As her friend and hostess, you want your friend to have a good time at your house, but it shouldn't be at the expense of humiliating someone else. If she won't listen to your reasoning and won't leave Hanna alone, remind her that cyberbullying could happen to her, too. If Hanna finds out that your friend was behind the nasty emails and comments, she might get back at her the same way. How would she like someone to do that to her? It could end up being a vicious circle. Also, explain that the two of you could also get banned from the Web site if they found out you had been involved in the trick. If your friend won't agree to leave Hanna alone because it's the right thing to do, she might leave her alone so that she won't get herself in trouble.

DILEMMA 25

Your friend saw a really cool model motorcycle kit that he wants to buy. He doesn't have enough money for it, so he wants to borrow the money from you. He says he'll let you help him build it in return for lending him the money. And he'll pay you back in three months.

Why is this a dilemma?

Your friend has a bad track record with you. Twice before he has borrowed money from you. Once he didn't pay you back at all, and the other time you really had to hassle him to get what he owed you. If you let him borrow the money this time, you might not get it back. And even if you do, you're likely to have to really hassle him again to get it. But if you tell him no, he might not like you anymore.

If you think of a solution, but it isn't a good one, what is the problem with that solution?

You could tell him you just don't have enough money to lend him, but you don't like lying to a friend. Besides, you're pretty sure he knows you do have enough money. You told him you were saving up to buy a video game system from another friend. You told him you almost had enough saved up, and he knows how much the friend wants for it. He certainly must know you have enough to lend him.

Is there a way around the problem?

You have to be pretty straight with him. He knows you have the money, so you're going to have to tell him that you just aren't willing to lend it to him. You have two choices for the reason you will give him. You can tell him it's because you don't want to lose out on the video game system. Or you can tell him it's because of your last two experiences in lending him money. If you tell him it's because of the video game system, you can add, "And think of all the fun you and I will have, playing those games together." That is a bit of salesmanship to make him want you to buy the video game system.

If he protests that he still wants the model motorcycle kit, you can tell him that you want the video game system just as badly. After all, you certainly have the right to buy yourself something you want, using *your* money.

He may still get angry for a while, but he shouldn't stay angry and stop being friends with you.

DILEMMA 26

Two of your friends are going door-to-door raising money for the "Elroy Animal Fund." But you know that there is no such thing as the "Elroy Animal Fund." "Elroy" is the name that your friends want to give to the rabbit they plan to buy when they've collected enough money to buy it.

Why is this a dilemma?

They are taking money from people and lying about what it's for. The people who give money think they are helping sick or stray animals. But really, the money is not going toward any such thing. It is going to buy your friends a pet rabbit. So, in a sense, your friends are stealing. Yes, collecting money and pretending it's for a charity, then keeping it yourself, is stealing.

Why is this a dilemma? Well, you know these kids are stealing. If you let them go on doing it, you feel like you're kind of guilty of something, too. After all, you know they're stealing from people and you're doing nothing to stop them.

If you think of a solution, but it isn't a good one, what is the problem with that solution?

You could tell them you know what they're doing and ask them to stop it. But chances are that they won't listen to you, and then they'll get angry with you, too.

You could let them go on doing what they're doing and decide to keep your nose out of it. But it's likely that at some point, people will find out what they've done. And when that happens, people may think *all* kids your age do stuff like that. And then there's this: When people find out that you knew and didn't try to stop your friends, the people may get angry with *you*, too.

Is there a way around the problem?

This is one of those dilemmas that you're better off getting a grown-up to help with. You can start at school. Tell your guidance counselor or the principal and see if they can help you. Because this illegal collection of money is taking place outside the school, they may choose not to get involved. But give it a try. The principal or guidance counselor might call the parents of the kids who are behind the scam. They might choose to have an assembly at which they explain why doing this sort of thing is wrong . . . and what kind of trouble you can get into if you do it. Or they may talk one-on-one with the kids who are involved.

Before you explain everything to the principal or guidance counselor, tell him or her that you don't want your name mentioned. Tell him or her that you don't want them to tell the kids who it was that told the principal or guidance counselor what was happening. This way you will be kept out of it, and your friends won't be angry with you.

PART 2

FAMILY DILEMMAS

DILEMMA 1

Your aunt has sent you an awful sweater for your birthday. Now your parents want you to write her a thank you note, and you don't know what to say.

Why is this a dilemma?

You don't want to lie and say you love the sweater, but you can't tell the truth in the thank you note and say you hate it.

If you think of a solution, but it isn't a good one, what is the problem with that solution?

You might think of asking your parents to thank your aunt for you. That way you don't have to say anything to your aunt. But you know you're supposed to write a thank you note yourself. And your parents wouldn't go along with you not writing one.

If you write your aunt and tell her you loved the sweater, not only are you lying, but she might send you more sweaters like it in the future. And what if she expects you to be wearing the sweater the next time she sees you? But if you say, "Too bad it's the wrong size and it's a terrible color," you're being honest, but you'll hurt her feelings.

Is there a way around the problem?

Can you find *anything* nice to say about the sweater? Without saying, "I really love the sweater you sent me," can you say it's a cheerful color?

Can you say it has an interesting pattern? Can you say it's a warm sweater? Can you say it was thoughtful of your aunt to remember your birthday? There you go — you've now said four nice things about the sweater and none of them is dishonest. You haven't actually said you *liked* the sweater. You haven't promised to wear it. And although you haven't told her how you honestly feel about it, you didn't tell any lies. The important thing is that you thanked her for the gift and for remembering you on your birthday.

DILEMMA 2

Your parents say you're all going to your grand-mother's nursing home for a visit. You love your grandmother, but you hate visiting her because she can never remember who you are. And where she lives is more like a hospital and smells like one too. You hate hospitals.

Why is this a dilemma?

You love your grandmother and you want to see her, and you know you should. But it's no fun to visit someone who doesn't even recognize you. And besides, hospitals freak you out.

If you think of a solution, but it isn't a good one, what is the problem with that solution?

If you have a lot of homework to do, or a big test coming up, your folks might excuse you from going. You could send your grandmother a little present with your family. She doesn't know who you are anymore anyway!

But you know it can't be fun to live in a place like that, and even if she doesn't remember who you are, surely your grandmother enjoys getting visitors and seeing friendly faces — and the more the merrier.

Is there a way around the problem?

If you *really* have a lot of homework or a big test to study for, it would probably be all right to stay home this time. But then you *really should go* next time. If you *don't* really have homework or study commitments, then go and see your grandmother. It might not be fun. It's probably not fun for your parents either. In fact, it might be even worse for your mom since Grandma is her own mother, and your grandmother probably doesn't recognize your mom either! But your mom goes to see her anyhow.

Your mom — and you — and the rest of the family can make the best of it and spread some happiness to your grandmother. You can hug and kiss her, talk to her, and make sure she's comfortable. You can bring her little gifts she'll enjoy. You can just be there for her and tell her a few stories about your week. In the larger scheme of things, it doesn't take that much time out of your day, and it can mean a world of difference to your grandmother's life.

Maybe try putting yourself in her position. If you were in a nursing home, wouldn't you want family to come visit and spend a little time with you?

DILEMMA 3

Your mom *always* asks you to watch your little brother. It seems as if you spend a lot of time staying home and keeping an eye on him.

Why is this a dilemma?

You like your little brother. He's a good kid. It's not that you actually mind watching your little brother. He's not that difficult to be with. He listens when you tell him something, and he really isn't too much of a handful.

It's just that whenever you have to watch him, it keeps you from doing anything else . . . like being with your friends. Lots and lots of times, you've missed out on having fun with your friends. It happens all the time. Your friends want to hang out and play soccer in the park at the corner, but you have to stay home and watch your brother. Two of your friends are getting together at the home of one of them. But you can't go because you have to stay home and watch your brother. A group of the girls are going to the skating rink. But you can't go. You have to stay home and watch your brother. It isn't fair!

If you think of a solution, but it isn't a good one, what is the problem with that solution?

Maybe if you did a bad job babysitting, your mother would stop asking you to do it. Then you'd get out of having to watch your brother all the time. But then your mom wouldn't be very happy with you. And maybe your brother would hurt himself in some way or damage the house if you didn't do a good job keeping an eye on him. That wouldn't be good.

Or maybe you could tell your mom that you have too much home-work to do and you just can't keep an eye on your brother and do your homework at the same time. And you need more time to do your homework.

In the first place, that would be dishonest. Not having enough time to do your homework is not what the real problem is. And in the second place, it wouldn't get you what you want: the chance to spend more time with your friends. Your mom would expect you to stay home and do your homework. And, after all, the whole point is to be able to spend less time watching your brother *so that you can spend more time doing fun things with your friends.*

Is there a way around the problem?

Have you talked to your mother about this situation? Does she realize how much time with your friends you're missing out on?

Maybe it can't be helped. Maybe your mother needs to work in the afternoons or on weekends, there's no one else to watch your brother, and Mom can't afford daycare or a sitter. On the other hand, maybe it's *not* necessary that you watch your brother so much. Maybe Mom just

— doesn't realize how much fun you're missing out on. And maybe she *could* make other arrangements, or stay home more, or take your brother with her when she goes out.

And maybe there is some middle ground here. Maybe Mom would let you have one friend over while you're watching your brother, as long as you and your friend were responsible about keeping an eye on your sibling. Or maybe Mom would give you a bigger allowance for watching your brother so often. Of course, that wouldn't solve the problem of how much fun you're missing. But it *would* give you something else to make up for it.

Try talking to Mom. If you're reasonable, not whiny or demanding or insistent, you have nothing to lose. The worst she can say is no.

DILEMMA 4

Somehow the back gate was left open, and your family's dog escaped. The city found him and picked him up, but when your parents got him back, he looked as if he'd been in a fight. He had cuts and bite marks all over him.

Not only was the dog hurt, but the whole thing cost your parents money. They had to pay the city to get the dog back, and then there was a bill at the vet's for treating the bites and cuts.

Your parents blamed you. They thought you

left the gate open when you brought your bike in and put it in the backyard. You were sure you had latched the gate behind you, but how can you prove it?

Then you went into your sister's room and saw that she'd left her diary out on the bed. Even though you knew you shouldn't, you picked up the diary and read it. In the diary, she wrote that she had left the gate open. You got blamed for what happened to the dog, but it was really your sister's fault.

Why is this a dilemma?

If you tell your parents what you read, you're admitting to reading your sister's diary. Then you'll be in trouble with them *and* with her. But if you don't tell them, they'll continue to blame you for what happened.

If you think of a solution, but it isn't a good one, what is the problem with that solution?

You could tell your sister that one of your friends saw her leave the gate open, and then she might admit it. But you know you're lying. Besides, if she challenges you, you don't really have a witness.

You could do something nasty or sneaky to get back at her. But your parents always tell you that "Two wrongs don't make a right," and besides, getting even doesn't really solve the problem.

Is there a way around the problem?

You really have only two choices: Admit you read the diary and get the mess straightened out; or keep your mouth shut, don't get in trouble about reading the diary, and keep on being blamed about the dog.

Wouldn't you rather be in trouble for something you *did* do than for something you're innocent of?

You should be honest and own up to reading the diary, and then deal with your sister's anger (and perhaps a few words from your parents about snooping). This way, at least you'll be cleared of the blame for what happened to the dog.

Maybe next time you won't read your sister's diary. Maybe next time your sister won't leave the gate open. Maybe next time your parents won't blame you so quickly. Maybe everyone will learn something from this unfortunate incident.

DILEMMA 5

Your mom and dad run a business from home, but sometimes they have to go out to see clients or run other errands. You have a house key, which you use whenever you get home from school and nobody else is home. Your dad told you last night that he and Mom would be out this afternoon and wouldn't be home until after 6:00.

You don't like being alone in the house for

that long. You get the idea that one of your friends could come over and play video games with you until he had to go home for dinner, and then you wouldn't be alone that long.

Why is this a dilemma?

You aren't supposed to have friends over unless one of your parents is there to supervise. And you know your parents aren't going to be home.

If you think of a solution, but it isn't a good one, what is the problem with that solution?

You and your buddy could do your homework instead of playing video games. Then it wouldn't be as if you had a friend over just to have fun. It would be more of a study session. And wouldn't your parents be happy to come home and find you've already done your homework without being asked?

Not really. You still had a friend over at the house when they weren't there. And that's really what they object to — not playing video games without supervision.

Is there a way around the problem?

You could ask one of your friends if *you* could go over to *his* house. Then call Mom or Dad on their cell phone and ask permission to go to your friend's house. If they say yes, and you can walk to your friend's house or get there by bike, that solves the whole problem!

DILEMMA 6

You're going to have a birthday party, and your parents say you may invite only ten friends. But there are twelve kids you're really friendly with.

Why is this a dilemma?

You don't want to leave two of your friends out. You don't even know how to choose which two to leave out. You don't want to hurt anyone's feelings.

If you think of a solution, but it isn't a good one, what is the problem with that solution?

You could tell your parents, "If I can't have all twelve of my friends, I don't want to have a party at all." Maybe they'll feel guilty and give in and then let you have all twelve over. But maybe it won't work. Maybe they'll say, "Okay, that's your choice." Then you won't get to have a party at all this year.

Is there a way around the problem?

Talk to your parents. Ask them, "Is it because of the expenses, or because supervising twelve kids is a lot of work?"

If they say it's the expenses, ask if you can compromise. Maybe if you agree to a less expensive kind of party, they'll agree to letting you invite all twelve friends. If your parents were going to take all of you to the roller skating rink, maybe you can just have a pizza party at home instead. If they were going to buy party favors for all the guests, maybe they can buy less expensive ones. If they were going to serve pizza, maybe they could serve just ice cream and cake.

If the problem is that they don't want to supervise twelve guests, maybe someone could help. Maybe one of your mom's or dad's friends or one of your friends' parents would be willing to be there to help.

It's worth asking and having a respectful conversation about. And who knows, the answer might be yes.

DILEMMA 7

You get a holiday gift from your uncle. It's perfect for you. It's an autographed picture of your favorite football player. Boy, even though your uncle lives halfway across the country, he really knows what you like! There's just one not-so-little problem: You already own an autographed picture of this player. One that looks exactly the same as the one your uncle gave you. You really don't need two that are alike!

Why is this a dilemma?

Your uncle obviously put a lot of thought into this gift — it's exactly what you love. But you already have one just like it. Now what do you do with the gift . . . and how do you thank your uncle?

If you think of a solution, but it isn't a good one, what is the problem with that solution?

You could ask him if he could exchange it at the store where he bought it. If he got it at a sports store, maybe he could trade it for a team jersey or something else that you don't mind having two of. Or something that you don't have at all. But you might hurt his feelings. He might feel bad to know his gift wasn't as perfect as he thought.

Is there a way around the problem?

Write to your uncle and thank him in BIG LETTERS with exclamation points!! Tell him how perfect the gift is for you. Tell him this athlete is your FAVORITE football player! Then try to trade the present with one of your friends. One of the other guys might want the picture and might have something you'd like in exchange. It might be something else having to do with football. It might be something completely unrelated to football. It could be a video game cartridge or a whole set of comic books. It doesn't matter. It's something you want — something your friend is willing to trade away for the picture. Now your friend is happy, you're happy . . . and your uncle is happy too!

Plus, you know you didn't lie to him at all in your thank-you note. (Bonus: If your uncle comes to visit and sees the picture hanging on your wall, he'll be thrilled to see it there. This is true whether it's the one he gave you or the one just like it that he didn't know you had.)

DILEMMA 8

Your parents are eager for you to get into a good university some day. Partly for this reason, they have you signed up for all kinds of classes and activities. You belong to a chess club, you're taking violin lessons, and you play soccer. Now they want you to learn another language.

Why is this a dilemma?

You have no interest in learning another language. You're really not interested in playing the violin either. You do enjoy playing chess at home with your friends and with your grandma, but you don't like having to show up once a week at a set time and play chess whether you feel like it or not. Soccer is the only one of these activities you really look forward to.

It feels like your days are too full. You have no time to just hang out anymore.

Plus, you want to be an agent for musicians when you're grown up. Musicians' agents don't need to know another language, or chess, or soccer, or even violin. And you don't have to get into an ivy league school to become a musicians' agent. But your parents tell you you'll change your mind twenty times before you start university. They tell you they know what's best for you. They insist you learn another language so that you can get into a good college someday.

If you think of a solution, but it isn't a good one, what is the problem with that solution?

You could deliberately mess up during your language and violin lessons. Maybe the teachers will tell your parents you're hopeless. Maybe the two teachers will tell your parents you'll never learn this new language or the violin.

But then your parents will probably just sign you up for some other courses instead. And your parents are likely to seriously get on your case about your inability to learn this language and the violin. Do you need that kind of hassle? And do they need to waste their money that way? (There's a lot of time being wasted, too, if you don't take your studies seriously or if you don't use what you learn.)

Is there a way around the problem?

Sit your parents down and tell them that there are two problems here. First, they are not leaving you any time to just relax and have fun. Second, they are enrolling you in courses you have no interest in. If they signed you up for stuff you really cared about, you would do much better in your classes. Explain to them that you need some time to just hang out and be yourself . . . and to do your homework, too. Also tell them you will learn much better if you are taking after-school classes you are really interested in. Find a class or two that really interests you, and offer to take that class instead of violin and the new language. Maybe you would like to learn music theory. Or maybe there are business courses that are open to kids your age. Or maybe learning the guitar would be better for you than learning the violin. If your parents see that you are really applying yourself in a different class, they might be happy with that.

DILEMMA 9

You told your parents you'd returned that library book, but the truth is you lost it. Now the library wants you to pay to replace the book, and you don't have the money for it.

Why is this a dilemma?

You can usually go to your parents when you need money for something legitimate. However, since you told your parents you'd returned the book, you can't ask them for the money now.

If you think of a solution, but it isn't a good one, what is the problem with that solution?

You could tell them you need the money for something else, something they'd approve of. But that would only make things worse because now you'd be telling them a second lie on top of the original lie.

Is there a way around the problem?

Go to the librarian. Tell her (or him) that you don't have the money, but that you're willing to work out your debt somehow. Tell her you'll do work around the library until you've paid off your debt in labor. Ask the librarian if that will be acceptable.

If it isn't, maybe you can earn money another way: rake leaves, shovel snow, pull weeds, walk dogs, and do similar chores (for pay) for neighbors.

Whether the library lets you work off the money or you're earning it through neighborhood chores, tell your parents either way. You need to be up front with them. Say to them, "You know that library book I told you I had returned? I guess I was wrong. The library says I never returned it. But I can't find it. So I'm working to pay them back."

And what if everything fails? What if the library won't let you work off what you owe them and you can't raise enough money by doing chores in the neighborhood? Well, you were going to tell your parents the truth anyhow. So tell them you want to earn extra money from them to pay the library back. Don't just ask them to bail you out. Ask them to advance you the money and to give you extra chores to make it up.

And then be sure to follow through on your promise. When your mom or dad asks you to rake leaves, to do laundry, to wash the dog, or to do some other extra chore to earn the money they advanced you, complete the task responsibly.

And don't forget to keep track of any future library books you take out. You might want to create a special corner or area in your room where you always keep your books — and be sure to mark the due date of each book on your calendar.

DILEMMA 10

You're watching the baseball playoffs on the TV in the family room. Dad is watching something on the other set. Your sister wants to watch a program in the family room. She says it's something she needs to watch for school. She says Dad is watching his favorite show so you'll have to let her change the channel.

Why is this a dilemma?

The baseball playoffs happen only once a year. And it's not as if you can catch them, months later, in reruns! You could go to Mom to complain. But you know she'll tell you to let your sister watch her show — it's part of her homework.

If you think of a solution, but it isn't a good one, what is the problem with that solution?

You could record the baseball playoffs and watch them tomorrow. But by then, all the other guys will be talking about the results in school. You'll know how the game ended. Watching it afterward won't be as much fun.

Is there a way around the problem?

You have several possibilities. One: Ask Dad if he'll let you watch the playoffs on the TV he's watching. When he understands that it's the playoffs, and how important they are to you, he might agree. Two: you can try to find the game on the internet or on the radio and then listen to it that way. Three: you can ask your parents if you can go to a friend's house and watch the game there.

DILEMMA 11

Your parents don't want you going into chat rooms or social networking sites online. They know the dangers that can come with conversations on some web sites. These can range from people simply talking about stuff that's inappropriate for kids your age, all the way to approaches from predators. Unfortunately, some adults who have bad intentions will often spend time in chat rooms and social networking sites that are of the most interest to kids.

Why is this a dilemma?

All your friends spend time in chat rooms and social networking sites. You don't like being the only one who doesn't. You want to see what everyone's talking about. You don't like feeling left out during conversations when all the kids at school talk about visiting these sites that you've never seen.

If you think of a solution, but it isn't a good one, what is the problem with that solution?

You could point out to your mom that "All the *other* kids go to chat rooms and social networking sites." But the "All the other kids do it" argument has never really worked with your parents before.

Or you could visit one of those sites when you're at the home of a friend whose parents don't object to his or her visiting those sites. If he logged on to the site and you just looked over his shoulder, it wouldn't exactly be as if *you* visited the site. Now you'd know what the other kids are talking about when they discuss these sites. But while you're not visiting these sites at home, and you didn't log on to the site yourself, you know you're fudging. While you didn't log on to the site yourself, and you didn't do it at home, you still could have been exposed to people with bad intentions, or people saying things you really shouldn't be reading.

Is there a way around the problem?

There are some chat rooms and social networking sites that are meant specifically for kids, and some in which conversations are monitored by a supervisor. Ask all your friends for the web site addresses of any chat rooms or social networking sites like these that they know about. Then give your parents the list. Ask them to check out some or all of the sites and see if they feel comfortable letting you go into them. You might also suggest that your parents talk with the parents of one of your friends who visits these kid-friendly sites and find out how they feel about the supervised sites. If your parents agree to let you go onto such a site, you can promise to let them read over your shoulder while you're on the site so they can see that nothing dangerous is going on.

DILEMMA 12

Your parents don't "live green." They throw away soda cans and other items that could be recycled. They bring home plastic bags from the store and wind up throwing them out. And they leave lights on when they leave the house and they keep the water running when they brush their teeth.

Why is this a dilemma?

You've learned about how important it is to "live green" and reduce, reuse, and recycle. But Mom and Dad say, "What one family does isn't going to make that much difference." You know that if everyone had that attitude, the world would soon be in a terrible mess.

If you think of a solution, but it isn't a good one, what is the problem with that solution?

You could find articles in the newspaper that talk about global warming. You could give these to your parents. But Mom and Dad already read the paper, or watch the news on TV. So they must know

about global warming. You could talk to them about the importance of "living green." But they might get annoyed with you for lecturing them.

Is there a way around the problem?

Maybe if you live green and *show* them (instead of just talking to them about it), they'll learn to be greener. For Mom or Dad's birthday, or another occasion, you could give them some big canvas bags to carry groceries in. Then they wouldn't use plastic bags anymore. You can promise to take the recycling bins to the curb on pick-up day if they'll start using the bins instead of throwing away cans, bottles, and newspapers. You can explain that doing little things day-to-day will help the environment (and can also make the monthly bills less expensive!). For example: turning off the lights when you're not in a room, turning off the faucet as you brush your teeth, hanging up wet clothes on a rack rather than using the dryer, turning down the heat and putting on a sweater, and taking shorter (and cooler) showers all add up for the environment *and* for the family funds. Maybe it's just a matter of showing them that little things can make a big difference.

Don't just tell your parents that they *should* live green. Tell them that you're worried about the world you'll have to live in by the time you're grown up. Don't just talk about what they *should* do, or what's good for the world. Make it *personal* and make it seem doable and realistic.

DILEMMA 13

Your parents bought you a new cell phone, and now you can't find it.

Why is this a dilemma?

This is the third cell phone you've lost. (And your parents even blamed you for the one that was stolen from your backpack. They said if you'd taken better care of it, nobody could have stolen it.) Your parents said they wouldn't replace this one if you lost it.

If you think of a solution, but it isn't a good one, what is the problem with that solution?

You could ask your grandma to buy you a new cell phone. She might do it if you don't tell her that your parents refuse to buy one for you. But your parents will find out you went behind their backs to Grandma. They'll say you were being sneaky and dishonest. Grandma will probably think so too. Then you'll be in trouble with all of them.

Is there a way around the problem?

You have to buy another cell phone with your own money or do without one. If you buy your own phone, you'll show your parents that you're taking responsibility for your actions. Then, the next time you lose something, they might not be as upset. (But try extra-hard not to lose this phone!) You do need to tell your parents that you've lost the phone. They're paying a usage fee for it. At best, they're paying for something you no longer have or use. At worst, someone else might be running up the bill and sticking your parents for it.

You can also ask your friends if any of them is on the same plan you are, and if they, or their parents or brothers or sisters, might be planning to get a new phone soon. Then you might be able to buy their old phone inexpensively.

When you do get a new phone, try keeping it on a lanyard, on a belt, or attached to you in some other way, rather than just carrying it in your pocket or in your backpack.

DILEMMA 14

Your parents are divorced. You see your dad every other weekend, and every other Wednesday. It's really great to see him! You miss him.

He tells you, "You're my helper now. I want to know everything that's going on in the family." And he asks a lot of questions.

Some of the questions are fine. He asks if the lawn is mowed, if you're doing your homework, if everything is okay at home. There's no problem there. But some of his questions make you a little uncomfortable. He asks about how your mom spends her evenings. He asks you if your mom is dating anyone.

You don't feel totally comfortable telling him. But he says it's nice to know he can count on you to tell him what's going on at home. Dad makes you feel important and grown-up. He tells you you're being a good son or daughter to him.

Why is this a dilemma?

You want your dad's approval. You like feeling important. But you don't feel right telling him your mom's private business. She isn't married to your dad anymore.

If you think of a solution, but it isn't a good one, what is the problem with that solution?

You could tell him what he wants to know. Your mom would probably never know you told him. And it makes you feel important, necessary, and helpful — as if your dad can really count on you. Isn't that a good thing?

But it also makes you feel as if you're letting your mom down. Aren't you being a spy? Aren't you telling your dad what your mom is doing in her private life? And you know that's not really your dad's business anymore. He's no longer married to your mom. He's still your dad, but he's not your mom's husband anymore.

Is there a way around the problem?

Explain to your dad that you won't tell him about your mom's private life . . . just as you wouldn't tell your mom anything about *his* private life. Tell him he's making this really hard on you and that you know you shouldn't carry stories from one parent to the other. Tell him you're doing well and so is your mom, and that the house is in good shape, but explain that if he wants to know about your mom's private life, then he needs to ask her, not you.

This might not be easy. But if you don't give him this answer, you're going to have him asking you questions about your mom all the time, and eventually that's going to be harder. You need to be firm and honest and explain to your dad how this makes you feel. It's likely that he knows he shouldn't be asking you about your mom, but he probably needs a firm answer from you in order to really realize it.

DILEMMA 15

Your parents don't make vegetables for dinner, but you've learned in school that you need lots of vegetables to be healthy.

Why is this a dilemma?

You'd like to ask your parents to serve vegetables at least a few nights a week. But you want to be respectful.

If you think of a solution, but it isn't a good one, what is the problem with that solution?

You could ask your parents to make lots of vegetables one night, and then you could split them up over a few dinners. But that means extra work for your parents — and you're not sure how good re-heated vegetables would taste.

Is there a way around the problem?

You could ask your parents if you could go with them to the grocery store next time. That way, you could take a look at all of the vegetables and ask someone working in the produce department what vegetables are in season and how to prepare them. You could also choose some colorful ingredients for a salad, and you could pick up some celery sticks to eat with cream cheese as an after-school snack.

This way, you help out with choosing the vegetables and preparing them. And who knows? Maybe your family will make eating vegetables a habit too!

PART 3

DILEMMAS WITH GROWN-UPS

DILEMMA 1

One of Mom's friends always likes to kiss you when she sees you. But she has bad breath and she squeezes you very tightly.

Why is this a dilemma?

Your mom expects you to be polite to all grown-ups, but this woman's breath is gross, and she has a grip like a boa constrictor. However, if you make a face and/or try to squirm away from her, your mom won't be very happy with you.

If you think of a solution, but it isn't a good one, what is the problem with that solution?

You could say, "Thank you, but I don't like to kiss people." But then she might say, "Aw, we're almost family, you can let *me* give you a kiss!" In that case, you could say, "Don't kiss me. I think I'm catching a cold," but that wouldn't be honest — and you can't use that excuse every time you see her.

Is there a way around the problem?

Yes, you can say, "If you don't mind, I'd rather shake hands." Shaking hands is an acceptable alternative. It's a very common greeting among adults and it keeps you at a safer distance. It also allows you to feel more comfortable with the exchange, while still being polite.

DILEMMA 2

Your mom and dad have been on your case about eating sensibly. They were both overweight for a while. Through dieting and exercising they both lost weight. But it was tough for them. They don't want you to have to go through what they went through. They tell you that being over-weight is unhealthy.

But when you're at your friend's house, your friend's dad offers you a brownie. At first you say, "No, thanks. I'll be having dinner in an hour."

But he insists. "I baked them myself," he says.

Why is this a dilemma?

You know your parents don't want you eating too much fattening food. And you know your parents don't want you eating an hour before dinner. But you don't want to hurt your friend's dad's feelings. After all, this isn't just any brownie. He baked it himself from scratch, and he wants to share it with you, which is really nice!

If you think of a solution, but it isn't a good one, what is the problem with that solution?

You could eat the brownie and then skip your next dessert to make up for it. But it's still an hour before dinner. You know if you eat the brownie now, you'll eat less dinner as a result. Eating sensibly isn't just about cutting way back on sweets and junk foods. It's also about eating enough of the right foods. And if the brownie fills you up, you won't eat enough of the dinner your mom or dad has cooked.

Is there a way around the problem?

You could say to your friend's dad, "I'm sorry, but it's too close to dinnertime. My parents wouldn't approve. But thank you. I *would* really like to taste your home-baked brownies, though. Would it be possible for me to take a brownie home with me to eat for dessert?" Your friend's dad will respect the fact that you're obeying your parents' wishes and you're being honest with him. He'll also feel good because you want to taste his baking. And he'll surely let you take a brownie home with you to eat later. (If it turns out that your mom has a special dessert planned, wrap the brownie carefully and save it for tomorrow. It won't get stale that fast.) And then be sure to tell your friend's dad how delicious the special treat was — and thank him again!

DILEMMA 3

Your older brother went to the same school you go to and had some of the same teachers you've had. Your brother is some kind of genius — really! He got straight As, was a science whiz, and absolutely amazed all the teachers and the principal.

But here's the problem: Your teachers (at least, the ones who had your brother in class when he went to your school) all expect you to do as well as your brother did. And they all say you can do better when you don't live up to the marks your brother got.

Why is this a dilemma?

You love your brother. And you're proud of him. But it can be a real pain to have all the teachers and the principal expecting you to live up to your brother's reputation. You're you! And it's not as if you're not trying! You're a good student and you really do study hard.

If you think of a solution, but it isn't a good one, what is the problem with that solution?

You could just give up trying. You're never going to equal your brother's accomplishments anyhow. You might as well have as much fun in school as you can. Forget competing with your brother's record.

But then you won't get good marks, and that could mess up your plans for the future.

Is there a way around the problem?

Talk to your guidance counselor. Explain to him or her that you cannot equal your brother's marks, no matter how hard you try. Tell him or her that you find it difficult to please your teachers because they expect you to live up to your brother's record. Ask if maybe you can be given teachers who never taught your brother.

Also try to find something you're particularly good at in school, and then do your best to excel in that subject. Perhaps you will even exceed your brother's record in that subject! This way, you can show your teachers that you are your own person and that you have your own strengths.

DILEMMA 4

An adult neighbor is cruel to his dog. You want to talk to him about it. Your friend says you had better mind your own business.

Why is this a dilemma?

You can't really tell a grown-up how to behave. Yet if you don't speak up to help that poor dog, who's going to?

If you think of a solution, but it isn't a good one, what is the problem with that solution?

You could leave a note for the neighbor and not sign it. Tell him you know he's cruel to the dog. Tell him you're watching him.

But if he's cruel and he finds out you're the one who wrote the note, he might do something to you, too. Or maybe, if he realizes a kid has left the note, he might just ignore it.

Is there a way around the problem?

In this case, you need to get help for the animal without getting involved with this neighbor directly. You need to tell one of your parents right away. Tell them what you have seen or heard and why you think the neighbor is abusing his dog. They can report this cruel neighbor to the SPCA (Society for the Prevention of Cruelty to Animals) or whatever local city or government agency would be the best to step in and do something to help protect the dog. Remember that cruelty to animals is serious and should never be ignored. But let your parents make the final decision about calling the SPCA or local agency. And let them make the phone call, too.

DILEMMA 5

Your basketball team practices three days a week after school. Because your mom and dad both work, your friend's dad drives you home from practice. But he smokes . . . in the car!

Why is this a dilemma?

You *hate* the smell of smoke, and you don't want your clothes and basketball gear to reek of it. It also makes you feel sick and you know it's not good for your lungs. You know that it's not just smoking that's dangerous — inhaling second-hand smoke is unhealthy too. But you're

not sure if you can really ask your friend's dad to stop smoking in his own car.

If you think of a solution, but it isn't a good one, what is the problem with that solution?

You can ride with the windows open and your face near the open window. But what if your friend's dad has the heater on in cold weather, or the air conditioner on in hot weather? Opening the window only works when the weather is mild and when it's not raining.

Is there a way around the problem?

You can try to politely ask your friend's father if he would mind not smoking during the drive home. You can explain that you are really sensitive to the smell and that it makes you feel sick to your stomach. Since it's only a short drive, and because you asked politely, your friend's father probably won't mind not lighting up while you're in the car (plus, he surely doesn't want you to get sick in his car!). It doesn't hurt to ask — he may not have known that cigarette smoke bothers you so much.

What if the smoke doesn't really make you feel sick to your stomach, but you still object to the smell and the second-hand smoke? Ask him, anyway. Leave out the part about getting sick, but tell him that you really don't handle the smell of cigarette smoke very well. If neither of your parents smokes, you might even add that your parents have asked you not to spend time in an enclosed space with someone who is smoking. (If they haven't actually said this, surely they will be glad to do so if you ask them to and if you explain why you're asking.)

DILEMMA 6

Your friend's mom has invited you to stay for dinner. But you discover – much too late – that she's serving your least favorite food. Or, even more serious, there may be reasons why you simply *can't* eat what your friend's mom offers you. Suppose you're allergic to tomatoes, which are in the salad? Suppose you're lactose intolerant, and the cauliflower was cooked in a cheese sauce? Suppose you're from a kosher Jewish or observant Moslem home and you can't eat the roast pork for religious reasons?

Why is this a dilemma?

If it's simply a matter of not liking the food, what are you going to do? Your parents have taught you not to say you hate foods — especially when someone else has cooked them for you. But you really don't like to eat fish, or liver, or lamb — whatever it is your friend's mom has prepared. And what if you really *can't* eat the food, for health or religious reasons? You still know your parents wouldn't want you to make a problem for your hostess — even though your parents wouldn't want you eating the food either. Allergies are very serious and you could get really sick if you eat the food in question.

If you think of a solution, but it isn't a good one, what is the problem with that solution?

If it's a matter of not liking the food, then you could try to force yourself to eat the lamb (or whatever the food is) anyhow. But if you have trouble getting it down, your friend's mom is going to notice. Then she might think it's *her cooking* you don't like, rather than *that particular food.*

If it's a matter of religion, then you could eat the pork and hope your religion would understand you were trying to be mannerly and not make problems. But you wouldn't feel right about it.

If it's allergies, you could eat the cheese or tomatoes (or whatever the food is) and hope you didn't have too bad of an allergic reaction. But should you really have to suffer in an attempt to have good manners? Eating food you're allergic to can be *very* dangerous.

Is there a way around the problem?

Yes, this is a case where honesty is the best — the only — policy. If it's a matter of disliking the food, you can say something like, "I'm sorry. I don't usually eat lamb. I don't really like it. But maybe I'll like the way you cooked it. May I try a very small piece first?"

At best, you'll find that your friend's mom *does* cook lamb in a delicious way. After you've tasted it, you can ask for a little more if you like it. Your friend's mom will feel flattered. If you don't like it, well, you've warned her you don't care for that particular food, so she shouldn't feel insulted if you don't have any more of it. As long as you don't make a face and say, "Oh, gross! I knew I didn't like lamb! Yuck!" you're not guilty of bad manners. Showing a willingness to try is polite.

DILEMMAS WITH GROWN-UPS

But what if it's a matter of an allergy or a religious belief? In either case, your friend's mom certainly will understand. If you say, "I'm sorry, but I'm not allowed to eat tomatoes. I'm allergic," or, "I'm sorry, but I'm not allowed to eat pork. We're kosher," then you're not being fussy, or difficult, or stubborn. It's important to speak up and make it very clear to your hosts if you have any food allergies. Food allergies can be very dangerous and no one wants you to get sick.

In fact, if you do have a food allergy, it might be a good idea to have your mom or dad call your friend's parents beforehand and say something like, "I appreciate that you invited Pat to have dinner at your house. I just wanted to make sure you knew that Pat has an allergy to tomatoes so that there won't be any tomatoes in what you're cooking. Thank you so much for understanding."

The key things to remember here are:

- Apologize for not eating the food that's a problem for you.
- Explain your reason briefly.
- Don't ask your friend's mom to cook something else for you. Eat whatever else she serves that you can eat, and have a nibble of something more when you get home if you're still hungry.

As long as you make do with whatever else your friend's parents serve — vegetables and potatoes, or soup and bread — you're not being a difficult guest.

DILEMMA 7

You'd like to learn to play the guitar, and your parents have agreed to pay for lessons. They suggested you ask the school music teacher for the name of a good guitar instructor. When you did, he strongly suggested you learn to play the flute instead. You have no interest in the flute. Your parents are okay with you learning the guitar. But the teacher insists the flute is a better instrument. What's more, he expects you to follow his advice because, as he says, "I'm an adult, and I know more than you do."

Why is this a dilemma?

You've been taught not to disobey adults. You've been taught not to hurt someone's feelings. By not taking his advice, at the very least, you might hurt this man's feelings. It also might be considered rude and/or disobedient. But yet you *know* that what he's told you to do is not the best advice for you.

If you think of a solution, but it isn't a good one, what is the problem with that solution?

You could tell him, "Thanks. I'll remember what you said," and then do what you know is best anyhow.

There are two problems here. One is that maybe, while his suggestion isn't a good one for you, your plan isn't the best one either. Some other instrument altogether might be a better fit for you. The other is that he might follow up and ask you, in a week or so, if you've started your flute lessons yet. *Then* what do you tell him?

Is there a way around the problem?

If this is not a situation where he expects you to follow his advice right then, you can always say, "Thank you for the advice," then discuss the situation with one of your parents (or another trusted adult who is knowledgeable about the subject). By getting another opinion from an adult, you accomplish two things. One: you might get a different opinion altogether — and one that feels right to you. Two: If the music teacher asks you later whether you've started your flute lessons yet, you'll have a better answer for him. You can say, "I spoke to my parents about it and they really want me to learn guitar," or "My sister's piano teacher thinks I'd be good at the cello, and I'm going to try that instead." This way, you're taking his advice into consideration and are doing what's best for you.

PART 4

EVERYDAY DILEMMAS

DILEMMA 1

Your teacher asks you to stay after school and talk to her about the trouble you're having in your history class. But she is called to the office just as she sits down. She tells you she'll be right back. You are standing right in front of her desk, and you can see that the test for tomorrow is right there. If you peek, you'll know what the questions and answers are!

Why is this a dilemma?

If you know what the questions and answers are, you can get a better grade — and you need all the help you can get! But you know you're not supposed to peek at the test.

If you think of a solution, but it isn't a good one, what is the problem with that solution?

If you only look at what the questions are and if you don't copy the answers, somehow it doesn't seem as bad. You could get the answers to the questions out of your textbook later on, and then you'd actually be learning something . . . so isn't that a *good* thing?

But you know you aren't supposed to peek. It's still a form of cheating. And none of the other kids knows what the questions are, so you'd have an unfair advantage.

Is there a way around the problem?

Honesty is the only answer. As tempting as it might be to peek, you mustn't. If you do badly on the test, at least you'll know you were honest. If you do well, you'll have gotten the good mark fairly.

And if you cheat, then get a good mark this once, and then do badly again on the next test, the teacher might suspect something. She just might remember you were alone in the room while the test was sitting there on the desk.

DILEMMA 2

There's a girl in your class who uses a wheelchair. Mom says to always be sensitive to and considerate of people who have disabilities. Trouble is, you really don't like this girl. It has nothing to do with her wheelchair – you've just found that she isn't a very nice or interesting person. You don't have anything in common with her. One day, she asks you over to her house after school.

Why is this a dilemma?

If you say no, she might think it's because of her disability. But the truth is, you really just don't want to be her friend.

If you think of a solution, but it isn't a good one, what is the problem with that solution?

You might decide to go over to her house this once and bring a friend. You could plan to spend more time with the friend than with the girl who invited you, and then you could leave early.

But, in the first place, she might expect you to invite her to your house next time. In the second place, if you and your friend spend more time with each other than with the girl whose house it is, she's going to feel more left out than ever. You will really hurt her feelings this way.

Is there a way around the problem?

There's a difference between being considerate of someone and pitying them. This girl doesn't want your pity. She wants your friendship. And apparently she isn't a great person. If you went to her house, it would be out of pity, not out of genuinely liking her. So, you'll have to gently tell her "No thank you" — that you don't want to go over to her house after school.

But be nice to her in school. You don't have to be friends with her. Friendship shouldn't be based on pity. Just be sure you're considerate of her in school and never do anything that could leave her thinking you're avoiding her because of her disability.

DILEMMA 3

The gym teacher always puts this one guy, who is the slowest runner, or the worst player, on your baseball team. It seems you just can't win with him on your team.

Why is this a dilemma?

You want to win but it's impossible with this kid on your team. You don't like losing all the time.

If you think of a solution, but it isn't a good one, what is the problem with that solution?

You could complain to the teacher that it's not fair for you to always be stuck with this guy on your team. But if the guy hears you complaining, his feelings will be hurt.

Is there a way around the problem?

There are at least two possibilities:

One is to talk to the teacher sometime other than during gym class. Point out that the teacher *always* puts this boy on your team and that this makes it very hard for you to win. Without whining, explain to the teacher that the game is much more fun when there's a fair chance of winning and that under these circumstances you have very little chance. The teacher may not even be aware that he always puts this boy on your team.

The other possibility is to try to help the bad player become better. If he's a slow runner, there's not too much you can do about it, but maybe the problem is that he's not very good at throwing or catching or batting. If that's the case, you can try to help him improve his skills. Give him some pointers. Practice with him. Help him. Maybe he needs to learn more about how to do something better, or maybe he just needs some extra encouragement. Maybe he really *wants* to be a better player but doesn't know where to start. He probably doesn't enjoy being the worst player.

If you help him improve his game, you're not only solving your own problem — you're doing a nice thing for someone else.

DILEMMA 4

Your parents ask you to do a load of laundry as soon as you finish your schoolwork. You say you will and you go upstairs to do your homework. But you need to call one of your friends to ask a question about an assignment, and in the process, you start talking about something else. Pretty soon, forty-five minutes go by.

You're upstairs and your parents are down-stairs. They don't realize you've been on the phone at all. You finally start to do your homework. But then you get distracted checking your email. You find a message that has to be answered right away. After awhile, you realize it's getting really late.

You log off and get back to your homework. But by now it's almost your bedtime. Your mom sticks her head in the door and says, "Still doing your homework, honey? I didn't know you had that much. Don't worry, I'll do the laundry for you."

Why is this a dilemma?

You got out of doing a chore and now your mom's doing it for you — but it all happened through a bit of dishonesty. Your mom thinks you were doing homework all that time, and you weren't. You didn't tell any lies, but you also didn't speak up and tell the truth.

If you think of a solution, but it isn't a good one, what is the problem with that solution?

You could go downstairs and tell your mom, "I wasn't doing my homework the whole time. I got distracted by a phone call and checking my email. I'll do the laundry right now."

She might be angry with you for not getting everything done in time and goofing off before your work was finished. And since she wants you to go to bed on time, she probably won't let you do the laundry anyhow.

Is there a way around the problem?

You can go downstairs and tell her honestly, "Listen, I have to tell you something. I had to call a friend to ask a homework question, and we got to talking — and that's part of why my homework isn't done yet. I know that was wrong. I also know it's too late for me to do the laundry tonight, but I owe you one. I'll do the laundry the next time you want it done. I promise. I'm sorry."

Your mom will respect your honesty and she probably won't get on your case big-time about goofing off when you should have been working. And you'll have a clear conscience. Just remember to follow through and help with the laundry — or another chore — next time.

DILEMMA 5

It's holiday time and your class is having a gift exchange. Everyone draws someone else's name out of a bag. Nobody is supposed to know who got whose name. You got Tara.

Nobody likes Tara. You don't really dislike Tara, but you're certainly not her friend. You think about giving her something disgusting. Wouldn't it be hilarious if Tara opened her gift and found plastic doggy poop? Fake vomit? Or something equally funny?

Even if nobody knows it was you, everyone will laugh. And if you tell some of the other kids that it was you who gave Tara the plastic poop, you know you'll be more popular than ever. Even if you don't tell them, your good friend Pam knows you got Tara's name. So Pam might tell the others that it was you who played the trick on Tara.

Why is this a dilemma?

You know that the rest of the kids will cheer you on for giving Tara a gross present in the gift exchange. But you also know that it's not nice to give such a present.

If you think of a solution, but it isn't a good one, what is the problem with that solution?

You can give Tara a serious present, a nice present, but your friend Pam knows that you drew Tara's name in the gift exchange, and Pam keeps urging you to give Tara something disgusting. "Won't it be so perfect when she opens the gift!" Pam keeps saying. You want Pam's approval. But do you really want to do something that is going to embarrass Tara?

Is there a way around the problem?

Put yourself in Tara's shoes. Would *you* like getting plastic dog poop or some other disgusting gag gift — especially in front of everyone? Why do something mean to her?

You don't have to spend lots of money and get Tara the nicest present in the store. Get her a little gift that you would like to receive. Being kind is the only answer in this situation. If Pam says anything to you, explain that you'd rather not make Tara the butt of a joke — especially around the holidays. Remind Pam that a little kindness — around the holidays and always — goes a long way.

CONCLUSION

Getting a Handle on Other Dilemmas

Now you have lots of ideas about how to handle some of the difficult situations you might face in your life. But even more than that, you've learned how to think them through. This will help you with *other* difficult situations. If you find yourself in a dilemma that I haven't described here, you'll be able to think your way through it by asking yourself:

* What is the problem?
* What are some possible solutions?
* What might be wrong with those solutions?
* What might be a better solution?

Use your head. Think creatively and you can think your way through many dilemmas in life. And nobody gets the answer right to *every* dilemma all the time.

Finally, here's one last — and much bigger — dilemma. Read on carefully.

> You become aware of a problem that you really feel needs to have something done about it – and yet you really don't know what to do. If you do the wrong thing, you and/or someone else could wind up with a bigger problem on your or their hands. Do you try to speak out or do something anyhow? If so, what? Or should you just try to forget the whole thing? Now you're *really* in a

> dilemma and you *really* don't feel comfortable simply ignoring the situation.

Maybe your gut instinct is telling you that you just can't find a way to fix the problem yourself. If you try, you might make things worse for someone . . . or you might get yourself into a really difficult or even dangerous situation.

Take a look at the different dilemma scenarios below. In each of these cases, you feel someone needs your help, or a bad situation needs reporting, or you have important information that needs to be given to someone who's in a better position to act than you.

What to do?

First of all, what types of situations am I talking about? I'll give you a few examples, though that's all they are — examples. There are certainly plenty of other such situations that would fall into the same category.

Situation 1

The kid next door is older than you, so you're not really friends. One day, when you're in your backyard, you see him sneak onto the screened-in back patio of a neighbor's house. He doesn't realize you're watching, but you see him steal a laptop computer or a video game system from that neighbor's house.

Since you have no real friendship with this kid and he's older than you, you don't think it would do much good to go up to him and say, "I saw what you did. Now put it back." Besides, if he's the sort who would steal, he might also be the sort who would do something nasty to you. On the other hand, if you just ignore the whole thing, someone's going to be without their computer — and all the valuable files and data on it. Replacing the computer would be expensive. Replacing everything on the hard drive would be totally impossible. Or maybe the video game system is something you know the kid next door saved up all his allowance to buy and it means everything to him.

Situation 2

Your best friend, Barry, tells you that his football coach has been inviting some of the team members over to his house. At first you think it's great that the coach is so cool. But after awhile, some of the things Barry tells you don't sound right. Maybe the coach is inviting the guys over one by one, not as a group. Or maybe he's been asking them some rather personal questions. Or maybe Barry says that the coach has a habit of touching him often — a bit more than you think is appropriate. Whatever the exact information is you're getting, you're not comfortable with it. And yet the coach hasn't done anything that very clearly crosses the line between friendly and just plain wrong. What to do? Suppose he is just being friendly? If you report him, you'll probably get him in BIG trouble . . . maybe for no reason. (Who would you report him to anyhow? And what would you report? He hasn't done anything clearly wrong.) Yet you know something about this situation feels all wrong, even though Barry might not agree with you. And you don't want Barry — or any of the other guys — to have to deal with it by themselves if the coach *does* have intentions that aren't appropriate.

Situation 3

You're biking with a friend. A car comes along and grazes your friend's bike tire, knocking him to the ground. Fortunately, your friend is only bruised and scraped. He's eventually able to get up and ride home. But the driver of the car never stops to make sure he's all right.

You make a mental note of the car's model, the color, and even the first few numbers of the license plate. But now what do you do?

Situation 4

A kid in school keeps saying he wishes he were dead. He says he doesn't care if he lives or not; he doesn't enjoy life anyhow, he says. You're afraid he might be thinking of killing himself, but you don't know this for a fact. You don't know his parents, either. You feel you ought to do something, but you haven't a clue what to do.

Situation 5

You notice one of your friends sometimes has bruises or other injuries. She's no longer willing to change clothes in front of you for gym class or when she comes to your house for a sleepover. You wonder if she's hiding more injuries. She says she just falls down a lot, runs into furniture, doesn't watch where she's going. But you wonder if someone is doing this to her. You'd like to protect her — if she needs protection. But you can't be sure – plus, she doesn't seem to want help. Yet, if you're worried that someone is hurting your friend, how can you let it go on without doing something? *What do you do?*

Situation 6

When your friend Melanie comes over for dinner, she excuses herself to the bathroom afterward. You're pretty sure you hear her throwing up. When she comes out of the bathroom, you ask if she's okay. She says she's fine. You don't want to embarrass her, so you drop the subject. And she seems okay for the rest of the evening. But another night, when you invite her over to dinner again, the same thing happens.

On both occasions, nobody else got sick to their stomach. You don't think it's a case of your parents serving something for dinner that had gone bad and made Melanie sick. And since it happened twice, and since Melanie was fine afterward, you don't think she had a stomach bug. What you begin to suspect is that Melanie made herself get sick on purpose.

You know some kids throw up intentionally after eating so they won't gain weight. But when you try to talk to her about it, she gets angry and tells you to drop it. She insists she's fine. She adds that if you're going to ask her any more questions like that, she's not coming over for dinner again.

You feel as if you should say *something* to *somebody*. But what can you do? You're not even sure you're right in what you suspect, which makes you even more uncertain about doing anything about it. Now what?

In each of these situations, you have to do something. Why?

- Because it's the right thing to do, morally.
- Because you have information that could help someone else — information that could save their lives in some cases.
- Because if it were *your* laptop computer (or your parents'), or your video game system, wouldn't you want to get it back? Because if the coach really is a child molester, do you want your best friend — or any other kid — to be his victim? Because if you were the person the hit-and-run driver injured, even though you weren't hurt badly, wouldn't you want the police to catch the guilty person? Don't you want them to make him or her go to court for what they did? And maybe take away their driver's license or make them pay a fine? Because if the boy who you think is suicidal does kill himself, his life is over — and his family is going to be going through unbelievable grief over it, too; there's no way to make things better after *that* happens. Because if the girl with the bruises really is being physically abused by a parent or someone else, she needs help — even if she's afraid to ask for it. Because if the girl who throws up after dinner has an eating disorder, she could make herself get seriously ill (or even die) if someone doesn't help her.

Okay, it certainly looks as if there are some serious reasons for not just turning your back and trying to forget you saw anything. But what should you do?

You need to do the same thing an adult does when he (or she) is in over his (or her) head — you need to *get help.*

Getting help can be as simple as telling a parent or some other adult.

Who are the adults you can go to for help with serious situations?

- Your parents
- Another close relative (an aunt or uncle, for example, or an adult brother or sister)
- A teacher, librarian, principal, or guidance counselor at school, or the school nurse
- A clergyperson (pastor or minister, rabbi or cantor, priest or imam)
- A police officer

If, for whatever reason, you feel you can't easily turn to any of these adults, you should find a well-known, respected organization that specializes in helping kids or in dealing with the sort of situation you're facing. Below, you will find some really useful phone numbers and Web sites of organizations that exist to help kids faced with really tough dilemmas. Be sure to keep these phone numbers and web sites handy. Remember: never be afraid to ask for help.

HELP!
(and where to find it)

Handy Hotlines and Web Sites

In an emergency, remember that you can always call 911 for immediate help.

All of the phone numbers listed here are free to call from a cell phone, pay phone, or home phone.

International

Befrienders Worldwide
www.befrienders.org

This is a Web site you can visit to get help with heavy issues, including: suicide, depression, self-harm, sexual orientation and gender identity, and bullying. Befrienders is based in London, England, but it has 205 support centers throughout the world. The Web site offers information in twenty-one different languages and provides an extensive directory of suicide and crisis help lines.

United States & Canada

Covenant House Nineline
http://nineline.org/
1-800-999-9999

This 24-hour bilingual (English and Spanish) hotline offers help "any-time, anywhere" for kids looking for answers to tough questions that deal with prejudice, family problems, alcohol, drugs, smoking, depression, and suicidal thoughts. People can call or email a counselor, ask a question through the site's special forum, search for help locally in the United States, or check out the site's content to learn more about the specific problems they may be dealing with.

Childhelp National Child Abuse Hotline
http://www.childhelp.org/
1-800-4-A-CHILD

This 24-hour help line is a confidential and anonymous way to get help in a crisis, ask questions about child abuse, and be referred to an organization in your area that can help. With the assistance of translators, the counselors are able talk to kids from the United States and Canada in one of 140 languages.

Canada

Kids Help Phone
http://www.kidshelpphone.ca
1–800–668–6868
Canada's only toll-free, bilingual (English & French), anonymous hotline has counselors available 24/7 by phone to listen to what's on your mind. You can also submit a problem via the Web site and a counselor will then read and respond within three to six days. The Web site has helpful information on bullying and cyberbullying, dating, friendships, family life, school, violence, abuse, and more. The Link Library provides a ton of resources related to all kinds of issues, and the Express Yourself page lets you write anonymous letters, browse what other people have to say, and add your own thoughts to the mix.

Teen Touch
http://www.teentouch.org/copingseries.asp
1–800–563–8336
The 24-hour help line can only be accessed if you are calling from Manitoba, Canada, but the Web site is for everyone. The Web site offers a "Coping Series" with information on subjects such as bullying, dating, moving, stress, and studying.

United States

Boys Town
http://www.boystown.org/
1-800-448-3000

Don't be fooled by the name — this organization has been helping boys *and* girls (and their families) for decades. Available 24/7, Boys Town urges people to "Call with any problem, any time." Callers are connected with a trained counselor who can provide assistance in English or Spanish or in one of 140 languages. With a database of over 20,000 agencies and services across the United States, Boys Town can refer you to a group in your community and provide follow-up support afterward.

Internet Resources:

FreeVibe
http://www.freevibe.com

This site provides information and free resources on the facts, myths, and little-known information surrounding alcohol, street drugs, and the abuse of prescription drugs. Visitors to the site can respond to polls, offer opinions, read celebrity news, and join online discussions. You can find stories about the impact drugs have had on the lives of real kids, and see what hundreds of thousands of teens call their "anti-drug." FreeVibe also has information on what you should do to help a friend who is using drugs or is thinking about using them. See what other kids are saying about drugs, violence, and the benefits of living drug-free.

Net Smartz Kidz
http://www.netsmartzkids.org
This Web site provides a ton of information about how to be safe online and what to do if something you come across online makes you uncomfortable or scared. Visit this site to learn about internet privacy, safe instant messaging, computer viruses, and more. While you're on the site, you can play games, take part in activities, and get free stuff, such as wallpaper, audio files, and screensavers.

Talk Helps
http://www.talk-helps.com
Take part in this Web site's interactive virtual playground and learn about bullies and the consequences of their behavior. You can also learn more about what it's like to be in someone else's shoes — the victim, the bystander, the person who intervenes or steps in — when faced with bullying. This site also helps you make a private online profile that will help you document the things and people that make you happy and sad.

KidsHealth
http://www.kidshealth.org/kid/
KidsHealth provides a "Dealing With Feelings" section that includes helpful insight into many different areas, such as cheating in school,

gossiping, bullying, peer pressure, alcohol abuse, divorce, having a crush, and even gift giving. This Web site also features fun games, videos, experiments, and activities.

It's My Life
http://pbskids.org/itsmylife/
Visit this site to get insight into a ton of topics, including sibling rivalry, going away to summer camp, being home alone, having a crush, making money, and much more. You can print off pages to help you create a personal journal, check out recommended books, play games, read celebrity interviews, and ask any burning question you might have. You can even give advice to parents who want help from kids!

Author and editor Cynthia MacGregor has written over fifty books for young readers and their families, including *Come on, Mom! 75 Things for Mothers and Daughters to Do Together* and *When I Grow Up, I Want to Be a Writer* (Lobster Press). Cynthia lives in Palm Springs, Florida, does public speaking, and offers a free ezine that you can sign up for by writing to ezinedoesit@cynthiamacgregor.com.